SCHOLASTIC

15 Standards-Based Science Activities Kids Will Love!

by Julie Fiore and Gwenn Lei

New York ● Toronto ● London ● Auckland ● Sydney

Mexico City ● New Delhi ● Hong Kong ● Buenos Aires

Teaching Resources

Acknowledgments

We could not have done this book without the
help of our friends, family, colleagues, and students:

To Lisa Frothingham, our mentor and friend,
who taught us everything we know

To Taylor Middle School staff and students

To Natalie and Gracyn, who encouraged us to
continue to provide quality education for our
future generations

To our families

Cover design by Brian LaRossa
Interior design by Kelli Thompson

ISBN 0-439-26274-7
Copyright © 2006 by Julie Fiore and Gwenn Lei
All rights reserved.
Printed in the U.S.A.

3 4 5 6 7 8 9 10   40   13 12 11 10 09 08 07 06

Table of Contents

Introduction

Welcome to *15 Standards-Based Science Activities Kids Will Love!*

As middle-school science teachers, we believe in fostering a love for science early in a student's academic career. We continuously refine our curriculum, looking for ways to pique students' curiosity and increase their motivation. Throughout the years we have found that fun and innovative projects help do just that, in addition to developing students' critical-thinking skills and strengthening their understanding of science concepts. We are fortunate to be located in an area rich in resources, enabling us to pull ideas from a variety of sources and colleagues. In turn, we have shared our ideas for student projects at professional conferences and discovered that other teachers love them too. In fact, they encouraged us to publish our ideas, and so this book was born.

Inside this book, you'll find a collection of engaging, classroom-tested activities and projects designed to motivate students and to help them display their learning in fun, creative ways. Students build space models, publish teen health magazines, videotape science informational shows, create comic books, and more. Some of these activities require only a couple of class periods to complete, while others span a few weeks. With long-term projects, we help pace students by assigning parts of the project for homework and occasionally setting aside class periods when they can work solely on their projects.

It would be fairly difficult to complete all of these projects within one school year, so pick and choose which ones you would like to do this year. You'll find that many of these projects lend themselves to other curricular areas, such as math or writing, and that they can be easily modified for English language learners and special-education students.

How the Activities Are Organized

Each activity includes the following: ───────────────

Overview—a brief background on the activity and its purpose

Science Standards—correlations to national and state science standards (The "New Teen Health Magazine" activity provides health standards.)

Materials—things you need to gather for the activity

Time Frame—a general idea of how long the activity should take (We based these completion times on a 50-minute class period. You should gauge your students' progress and adjust time as necessary.)

Getting Started—suggestions for introducing the activity and getting students started on their work

Tips—helpful management tips to make the activity run more smoothly

E ach activity also includes a reproducible student handout that fully explains the project's goal and includes step-by-step instructions on what students need to do. A couple of activities also come with extra reproducibles, such as a writing frame or a planner, to help students complete their work. We've also included grading rubrics for each project so students have a clear understanding of your expectations and how their work will be graded. At the back of this book, you'll find additional rubrics for grading students' homework and lab report.

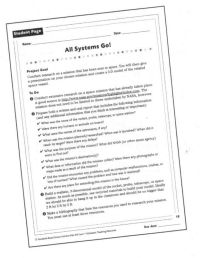

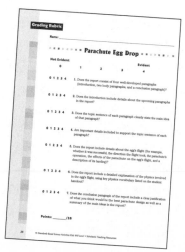

We hope that you find our ideas useful and that your students enjoy the work along the way. We believe students' final products set these assignments and projects apart. Remember to save the best work from each year to use as models, and you'll see the quality of student work improve each year. Enjoy!

Welcome-to-Science Collage

Overview

This beginning-of-the-year project offers the perfect opportunity for students to get to know each other and to understand how they behave like scientists in their everyday lives. As students put together their collage, they discover that science is all around them and encompasses many areas of their life. This is a great activity for the first days of school, resulting in a project that can be displayed for Back-to-School night.

Science Standards _____

✓ understands the nature of scientific knowledge
✓ understands the nature of scientific inquiry
✓ understands the scientific enterprise

Materials

⦿ student handout (page 7)
⦿ 12-by-18-inch construction paper
⦿ glue
⦿ scissors
⦿ magazines (students can bring in to cut out)
⦿ markers and/or color pencils

Time Frame

One to two class periods, depending on whether you want students to complete this project at home

Getting Started

Ask students: *In what ways does science affect your life?* List students' responses on the board. If necessary, provide students with examples of science in everyday life, such as chemistry used to create hair gel or the physics of safety belts.

Next, invite students to think about different kinds of scientists and the skills that they use: observing, predicting, classifying, measuring, calculating, experimenting, asking questions, analyzing data, drawing conclusions, communicating, developing hypotheses, sharing information. Encourage students to think about how they might be using these same skills at home and at school.

Tell students that they will be creating a two-sided collage. Just like many back-to-school projects, the first side of the collage will be all about themselves. Using magazines, students will cut out pictures that reflect who they are, what they like to do, and so on. The second side of the collage will show how science relates to their own lives. Remind students about the skills scientists use, and challenge them to think about when and how they use these skills in their daily lives.

Distribute the student handout and collage materials. Encourage students to fill in the information on the handout before they start working on the collage.

◆ ◆ ◆ ◆ ◆ ◆ ◆ ◆ Tips ◆ ◆ ◆ ◆ ◆ ◆ ◆ ◆

⦿ Circulate around the room to make sure students stay focused on finding specific items for their collage. Students can sometimes get caught up in reading the magazines.

⦿ This project can easily be finished in two sessions. Encourage students to pace themselves so that they can complete one side of their collage per session. Allow plenty of time for cleanup.

15 Standards-Based Science Activities Kids Will Love! • Scholastic Teaching Resources

Name: _____ **Date:** _____

Welcome-to-Science Collage

■ ■

Project Goal
Create a collage that tells about yourself and how you use science in your everyday life.

To Do

❶ Plan your collage by filling out the information below.

❷ On a sheet of construction paper, sketch out a large science-related shape, such as a magnifying glass, beaker, or star. Cut out the shape.

❸ Look through magazines to find pictures, illustrations, or words that reflect your answers below. Cut them out and glue them to your construction-paper shape.

Side 1: All About Me

I am _____

I like (or my favorite things are) _____

People like me because _____

I am good at _____

Here are other things you should know about me: _____

_____

_____

Side 2: Science and Me

I am a scientist at home when I _____

I am a scientist at school when I _____

I like science because _____

If I could be any type of scientist I would be _____

Science helps people _____

Note: Think about the skills that scientists use, such as observing, predicting, classifying, measuring, calculating, experimenting, posing questions, developing hypotheses, analyzing data, drawing conclusions, communicating, and sharing information.

15 Standards-Based Science Activities Kids Will Love! • Scholastic Teaching Resources

Due date: _____

Pop-Up Resource Book

Overview

Students hone their Internet research skills as they investigate the science behind a particular topic of interest. They will synthesize information they gathered into a three-dimensional pop-up book.

Science Standards

✓ understands the nature of scientific knowledge

✓ understands the nature of scientific inquiry

✓ understands the scientific enterprise

Materials

- student handout (page 9)
- Web Site Evaluation Rubric (page 10)
- construction paper
- scissors
- glue
- children's pop-up book (to use as a model for making a pop-up book)

Time Frame

This is a long-term project in which students do most of the work outside of class. If possible, block out 3 to 5 days at the computer lab for research.

Getting Started

Help students brainstorm a list of topics they're interested in (e.g., music, movies, videos) and discuss the science behind them. For example, if the topic is music, students could research the physics of sound. You may need to assist them in drawing a relationship between their topic and science.

Inform students that they will be conducting research about their chosen topic on the Internet. Remind them to take good notes about their topic and keep a list of Web sites they visited. Encourage students to visit at least five sites and evaluate each site for accuracy, currency, and balance. Distribute copies of the Web Site Evaluation Rubric. Caution students against visiting suspicious sites.

Next, inform students that they will produce a pop-up book showing what they've learned. Each pop-up book should contain five pages, with each page dedicated to either an annotated Web site or a category of the topic. Show students a children's pop-up book, then demonstrate how to create a simple pop-up page: Fold a piece of construction paper in half, then cut two parallel slits about an inch apart and 2 inches long into the fold (see illustration on page 9). Open and pop out the resulting "pedestal" and glue a picture or piece of information on it.

◆◆◆◆◆◆◆◆ Tips ◆◆◆◆◆◆◆◆

- Let students pick their own topic. Students tend to be more motivated and produce better work when they choose a topic they are interested in. Ask students to choose different topics so that there is no repetition within a class.

- Be sure to keep good examples of students' pop-up books for next year. You'll notice that as your samples get better so does the quality of the work students produce.

---

15 Standards-Based Science Activities Kids Will Love! • Scholastic Teaching Resources

Name: _____ Date: _____

Pop-Up Resource Book

■ ■

Project Goal

Uncover the science behind a topic that interests you. After choosing a topic in class, conduct research on the Internet about your topic and then create a pop-up book to show what you learned.

To Do

❶ Choose a topic that you find interesting, and conduct research on the Internet to discover the science behind it. Make sure to take careful notes and list your sources. (Evaluate each Web site using the evaluation rubric from your teacher.)

❷ Based on your research, create a pop-up book that includes the following:

✔ attractive cover page that clearly states the topic, your name, and class period

✔ 5 pop-up pages, with a different science connection on each page (each page should be detailed and colorful and should include at least one picture)

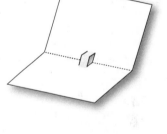

✔ summary page explaining:

a) why you chose this topic

b) in what way your topic affects society

c) how completing this project has changed your view of science

✔ bibliography with at least five resources (Web sites you used to get your information)

❸ To create a page for your pop-up book, fold a piece of construction paper in half. Next, cut two parallel slits about an inch apart and 2 inches long into the fold. Open and pop out the resulting "pedestal" and glue a picture or piece of information on it.

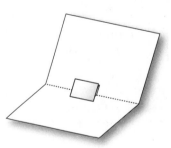

Example: ─────────────────────────

Topic: Dogs

Page 1: Anatomy   **Page 4:** Genetic Disorders

Page 2: Reproduction   **Page 5:** Breeding

Page 3: Acute Dog Senses   **Page 6:** Summary and Bibliography

Due date: _____

Name: _____ Date: _____

Web Site Evaluation Rubric

■ ■

Grade aspects of each Web site on a scale from 1 (lowest) to 5 (highest).

Web site/URL: _____

CRITERIA	SCORE
Accuracy—Is the content on the site accurate and reliable? (If the content is written by notable experts, it is most likely accurate.)	1 2 3 4 5
Currency—Is the information on the site up-to-date? (Some sites show when they were last updated.)	1 2 3 4 5
Balance—Is the content written objectively? (In other words, are the authors trying to sway you toward their point of view?)	1 2 3 4 5

Web site/URL: _____

CRITERIA	SCORE
Accuracy—Is the content on the site accurate and reliable? (If the content is written by notable experts, it is most likely accurate.)	1 2 3 4 5
Currency—Is the information on the site up-to-date? (Some sites show when they were last updated.)	1 2 3 4 5
Balance—Is the content written objectively? (In other words, are the authors trying to sway you toward their point of view?)	1 2 3 4 5

Web site/URL: _____

CRITERIA	SCORE
Accuracy—Is the content on the site accurate and reliable? (If the content is written by notable experts, it is most likely accurate.)	1 2 3 4 5
Currency—Is the information on the site up-to-date? (Some sites show when they were last updated.)	1 2 3 4 5
Balance—Is the content written objectively? (In other words, are the authors trying to sway you toward their point of view?)	1 2 3 4 5

Due date: _____

15 Standards-Based Science Activities Kids Will Love! • Scholastic Teaching Resources

Name: _____

▪ ▪ ▪ ▪ ▪ ▪ Pop-Up Resource Book ▪ ▪ ▪ ▪ ▪ ▪

CRITERIA	SCORE
CONTENT Contains up to five specific connections to science. Each connection explains in detail the science behind the topic and shows a thorough understanding of scientific concepts. The report is written using student's own words, with science vocabulary used correctly.	(_____/50 points)
SUMMARY Clearly explains why student chose this topic and how the topic affects society. Also explains how working on this project has changed student's view of science.	(_____/10 points)
PRESENTATION Each pop-up page features at least one picture that supports the content on that page. Text on each page is legible with correct spelling and grammar. Each page is colorful and shows creativity.	(_____/30 points)
BIBLIOGRAPHY Lists at least five different resources (Web sites) from where student gathered information on the topic.	(_____/10 points)
TOTAL: _____/100 points	

Comments:

_____

_____

_____

Biographical Scrapbook

Overview

We do this project early in the year to expose students to a wide variety of careers in science. Students research a scientist and use the information to create a scrapbook of the scientist's life. We encourage students to choose scientists of color, women scientists, and even contemporary scientists.

Science Standards

✓ understands the nature of scientific knowledge
✓ understands the nature of scientific inquiry
✓ understands the scientific enterprise

Materials

● student handout (page 13)
● list of suggested scientists (optional)

Time Frame

About 3 weeks (All work and research should be done outside of class.)

Getting Started

If possible, create a list of suggested scientists from which students can pick (the Internet is a great resource). Or, have students do research to find their own scientist. We encourage our students to pick scientists off the beaten track—you'll certainly appreciate not getting 10 projects on Sir Isaac Newton. We have each student choose a different scientist so there is no repetition within a class. This way, there's less conflict when students look for reference materials in both local and school libraries.

Distribute the student handout and read through with students. Explain each requirement of the scrapbook. Emphasize that once they have done all the research necessary, they will virtually become that scientist and should create the biographical scrapbook accordingly.

◆ ◆ ◆ ◆ ◆ ◆ ◆ Tips ◆ ◆ ◆ ◆ ◆ ◆ ◆

● Pace students so they have adequate time and don't wait until the last minute to complete the project. We assign a rough draft of one of the requirements every other day for homework.

● Encourage students to be creative and get into the role of their scientist, especially for the journal entry.

● If students choose a living scientist, encourage them to contact the person via e-mail or phone, and add their interview to the scrapbook.

● For English-language learners and special education students, decide with each student which piece of the project to focus on and include.

Name: _____ Date: _____

Biographical Scrapbook of a Scientist

■ ■

Project Goal

Conduct research on a famous scientist and put together a scrapbook of his or her life. Your scrapbook should show evidence that you really learned something about the scientist and were able to compile the information in an interesting manner.

To Do

❶ Select a scientist from the teacher's list. If there is another scientist who is not on the list whom you would like to research, ask for some help. Make sure there is enough information available to help you understand the scientist you choose.

❷ Go to the library and conduct research on your chosen scientist. Keep a bibliography as you read. The bibliography should be in this form:
Author's Last Name, First Name. Title of Publication. Publishing Company, Date of Publication. Page numbers used.

Sample Bibliography Entry:
Smith, Sally. *The Life and Times of Albert Einstein.* Simon and Schuster, 1989. Pages 24–34.

❸ Use your notes to put together a scrapbook about your scientist. Your scrapbook must contain the following:

✔ title page—include the scientist's name, a picture or illustration, and your name

✔ introductory page—explain who the scientist is and why you chose him/her

✔ "mock" or fake birth certificate—include vital information, such as date and place of birth

✔ diary entry that the scientist may have written as a child—should reveal something about the person's childhood (e.g., where he grew up, went to school, and so on)

✔ "mock" newspaper article—report on a major event or achievement in the scientist's life

✔ time line—create a chronological representation of major events in this person's life (both scientific and personal)

✔ speech or essay written by your scientist on the following topic: "Advice to Young People Who Want to Succeed in Science"

✔ obituary for the scientist—a one-paragraph description that might appear in a newspaper after his or her death. Summarize the scientist's life history and include his or her accomplishments in science, education, work history, and names of spouses, children, and grandchildren, if any.

✔ additional information you might want to include, like an interview transcript

Due date: _____

Biographical Scrapbook

∎ ∎ ∎ ∎ ∎ ∎ ∎ ∎ ∎ ∎

Name: _____

Piece of Work	Points Possible	Points Earned
Title page	10	
Introduction	10	
Birth certificate	10	
Diary entry	10	
News article	10	
Time line	10	
Speech	10	
Obituary	10	
Bonus material	10	
Bibliography	10	
Total points	**100**	

Your score for each element of the scrapbook will be based on the following criteria:

● Information is factual and shows complete knowledge and thorough understanding of the scientist's life, accomplishments, and contributions to society.

● Each page is neat, attractive, and creative.

● Text is legible with correct spelling and grammar.

✂ -

Grading Rubric

Biographical Scrapbook

Name: _____

Piece of Work	Points Possible	Points Earned
Title page	10	
Introduction	10	
Birth certificate	10	
Diary entry	10	
News article	10	
Time line	10	
Speech	10	
Obituary	10	
Bonus material	10	
Bibliography	10	
Total points	**100**	

Your score for each element of the scrapbook will be based on the following criteria:

● Information is factual and shows complete knowledge and thorough understanding of the scientist's life, accomplishments, and contributions to society.

● Each page is neat, attractive, and creative.

● Text is legible with correct spelling and grammar.

New Teen Health Magazine

Overview

We use this project as a wrap-up assessment tool for our family-life unit. We begin by teaching about nutrition and spend a good deal of time focusing on self-esteem. Our students love working on this project where they get to be editors of their own magazine.

Health Standards

✓ knows environmental and external factors that affect individual and community health

✓ knows how to maintain mental and emotional health

✓ understands essential concepts about nutrition and diet

✓ knows how to maintain and promote personal health

✓ understands aspects of substance use and abuse

✓ understands the fundamental concepts of growth and development

Materials

● student handout (page 16)
● construction paper
● resources on health topics
● teen magazines

Time Frame

About 3 class periods (Have students do most of their writing for homework.)

Getting Started

Bring in some samples of teen magazines to the class. Hold up a magazine, showing students the model on the cover, and then flip through the pages to show other models inside as well. Ask students: *How do you think the media portrays ideal beauty? Do you think it's realistic?* Discuss some of the ways that media perpetuates unrealistic stereotypes and how this impacts the way

teens may perceive themselves. If necessary, review some of the topics you have covered in your health unit, such as nutrition, fitness, smoking, and more.

Divide the class into groups of 5 or 6 students. Explain to students that they will be working together in groups to create their own teen health magazine. Students will be held accountable individually and as a group. Each person is responsible for completing three pieces of work—an article, an advertisement, and a letter to the editor—to be included in the magazine. Students can choose from a wide variety of health-related topics, such as nutrition, fitness, self-esteem, peer pressure, eating disorders, drugs, alcohol, and tobacco. Remind students that all articles and advertisements should promote positive body image and lifestyle and be free of the usual stereotypes portrayed in typical teen magazines.

◆ ◆ ◆ ◆ ◆ ◆ ◆ ◆ **Tips** ◆ ◆ ◆ ◆ ◆ ◆ ◆ ◆

● Distribute real teen magazines to each group to give students ideas for articles and layout.
● Encourage students to include other magazine features, including horoscope, crossword, advice columns, and so on.

Name: _____ Date: _____

New Teen Health Magazine

■ ■

Project Goal

With your team, create a new magazine that promotes a healthy lifestyle for teenagers. All the images, pictures, advertisements, editorials, and articles in the magazine should promote a positive body image and healthy eating and fitness habits.

To Do

❶ Review your notes and any other resources your teacher may have handed out regarding teen-health issues.

❷ Come up with a table of contents for your teen health magazine and decide who will write each article. Each person in your team should write one article, one advertisement, and one letter to the editor. Articles and letters should be typed and proofread for spelling and grammar.

❸ As a team, decide how to design and lay out the magazine. Look at other magazines for some ideas. Cut out or draw pictures to help make your magazine look more realistic.

❹ Your finished magazine should include the following:

✔ An eye-catching, colorful, and attractive cover

✔ A table of contents

✔ 3 or 4 articles—must include information on eating disorders, nutrition, fitness advice, anti-drug, tobacco, or alcohol, and self-image/esteem issues

✔ Pictures on each page of the magazine

✔ 3 or 4 advertisements promoting healthy products and/or healthy body images, anti-drug, tobacco and/or alcohol issues

✔ 3 or 4 letters to the editor expressing an opinion about a particular teen-health issue

✔ A biography page about each author. Your biography page should tell about you, your hobbies, your health habits, and your role models. You may include a picture of yourself on this page.

▪ ▪ ▪ ▪ ▪ ▪ ▪ **Teen Health Magazine** ▪ ▪ ▪ ▪ ▪ ▪ ▪

GROUP SCORE: _____ / 100 points

Team Members: _____

_____

_____

Cover (_____ / 20 points)
Cover is attractive and eye-catching. The magazine's title is large and prominent. The cover highlights appealing articles and feature stories that will entice readers to pick up the magazine.

Table of Contents (_____ / 5 points)
Lists a variety of articles related to teen health, as well as thumbnail photographs related to the topics.

Articles (_____ / 25 points)
Cover a wide range of teen-health articles. Each member of the group has contributed one article that is well written and shows a thorough understanding of the topic. Each article includes a head (title) and byline (author's name). Text is typewritten and proofread for spelling and grammar. Photographs or other graphics support the text and are properly captioned.

Advertisements (_____ / 25 points)
Promote healthy products and/or a healthy body image. Each member has designed one advertisement that shows colorful photographs and catchy text.

Letters to the Editor (_____ / 25 points)
Address important issues and/or concerns related to teen health. Each member has written a letter that raises an important issue or concern. The letter includes details about the issue and expresses a well-informed opinion based on facts. The letter is legible with correct spelling and grammar.

INDIVIDUAL SCORE: _____ / 100 points

Student's Name: _____

Article (_____ / 50 points)
Article is well written and organized in a logical way. It contains factual information that shows a thorough understanding of the topic. Article is typewritten and proofread for spelling and grammar.

Advertisement (_____ / 25 points)
Advertisement includes colorful photographs and catchy text, promoting healthy products and/or a healthy body image. It shows evidence of a thorough understanding of the topic.

Letter to the Editor (_____ / 25 points)
The letter discusses an important teen-health issue and expresses a well-informed opinion based on facts. The letter is legible with correct spelling and grammar.

All Systems Go! A Space Mission Project

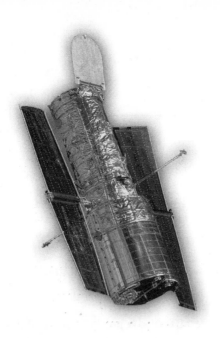

Overview

In this project, students will conduct research to become experts on a space mission. Students have an opportunity to focus on NASA's program or other countries' space programs.

Science Standards _____

✓ understands the composition and structure of the universe and the Earth's place in it

✓ understands the nature of scientific knowledge

✓ understands the nature of scientific inquiry

✓ understands the scientific enterprise

Materials

● student handout (page 19)

● resources on space missions (NASA is an excellent resource) or access to the Internet

● art materials and recycled items for building space models (Discourage students from buying spaceship models.)

Time Frame

3 to 5 days for research (in class or as homework), plus 2 class periods for oral presentations

Getting Started

Ask students to think about any space missions they may have heard about; for example, the *Pathfinder* mission to Mars or even the *Apollo 11* mission to the moon. Brainstorm a list with the class, adding any other missions you would like students to report on. (You may want to visit http://www.nasa.gov/missions/highlights/index.html for information on NASA's space missions.)

Explain to students that they will be working in pairs to complete this assignment. The project consists of three parts—a written report, an oral presentation, and a three-dimensional spaceship model. Go over the handout with students, making sure they understand the project requirements.

Remind students to include a bibliography that lists the resources they used to research their mission.

When making their models of a space rocket or probe, remind students to be creative, clever, and cost-effective in their construction.

◆ ◆ ◆ ◆ ◆ ◆ ◆ **Tips** ◆ ◆ ◆ ◆ ◆ ◆ ◆

● Consider pairing students who have different strengths so they can divide the work and play to their strengths.

● Review elements of a good oral presentation. Encourage students in the audience to take notes on their fellow classmates' presentations and offer constructive criticism to the presenters.

Name: _____ Date: _____

All Systems Go!

■ ■

Project Goal

Conduct research on a mission that has been sent to space. Then give a presentation on your chosen mission and create a 3-D model of the related space vessel.

To Do

❶ Conduct extensive research on a space mission that has already taken place. A good source is http://www.nasa.gov/missions/highlights/index.com. The mission does not need to be limited to those undertaken by NASA, however.

❷ Prepare both a written and oral report that includes the following information (and any additional information that you think is interesting or important):

✔ What was the name of the rocket, probe, telescope, or space station?

✔ Were there any humans or animals on board?

✔ What were the names of the astronauts, if any?

✔ When was the mission planned/researched? When was it launched? When did it reach its target? Were there any delays?

✔ What was the purpose of the mission? What did NASA (or other space agency) want to find out?

✔ What was (were) the mission's destination(s)?

✔ What data or information did the mission collect? Were there any photographs or maps made as a result of the mission?

✔ Did the mission encounter any problems, such as computer malfunctions, crashes, or loss of contact? What caused the problem and how was it resolved?

✔ Are there any plans for extending this mission in the future?

❸ Build a realistic, 3-dimensional model of the rocket, probe, telescope, or space station. As much as possible, use recycled materials to build your model. Ideally it should be no bigger than 2 feet by 2 feet by 2 feet.

❹ Make a bibliography that lists the resources you used to research your mission. You must use at least three resources.

Due date: _____

Name: _____

■ ■ ■ ■ ■ ■ ■ ■ All Systems Go! ■ ■ ■ ■ ■ ■ ■ ■

CRITERIA	SCORE
WRITTEN REPORT Includes all required information from the student handout. Information is factual, well researched, and shows a thorough understanding of scientific concepts. Bibliography lists all resources used for research. Report is neat and legible with correct spelling and grammar.	(_____/35 points)
MODEL OF ROCKET OR PROBE Is an accurate representation of the actual space vehicle used in the mission. Details in the model show evidence of careful research and planning. The model is made from recycled items and shows creative use of materials.	(_____/30 points)
ORAL PRESENTATION Information is presented in a clear, loud voice for everyone to hear. Visual aids, such as the 3-D model and photographs, are used to engage listeners and offer more specific details about the mission.	(_____/35 points)
TOTAL: _____/100 points	

Comments:

_____

_____

_____

_____

Great Parachute Egg Drop

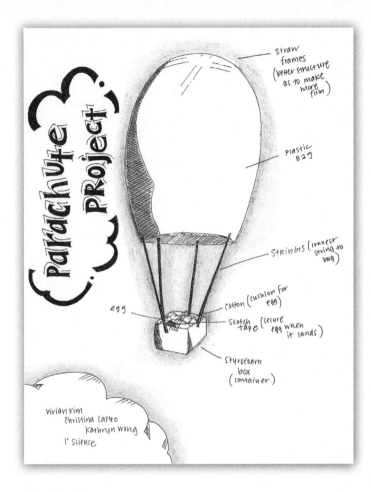

Parachute Project

straw frames (better structure as to make more firm)

plastic bag

strings (connect string to bag)

cotton (cushion for egg)

egg

scotch tape (secure egg when it lands)

styrofoam box (container)

vivian kim
Christina Castro
Kathryn Wong
1° science

knows the relationship between the strength of a force and its effect on an object

✓ understands general concepts related to gravitational force

✓ understands the effects of balanced and unbalanced forces on an object's motion

✓ understands the nature of scientific knowledge

✓ understands the nature of scientific inquiry

Overview

We use this activity as a final assessment of our physics unit. We challenge students to incorporate all relevant physics concepts into designing a parachute that will carry a raw egg safely to the ground. We supply the raw eggs and ask students to bring in materials to build their parachutes in class. You will need a place to drop your chutes. We use an area where the drop is about 5.5 meters.

Science Standards

✓ knows that an object's motion can be described by tracing and measuring its position over time

✓ knows that when a force is applied to an object, the object either speeds up, slows down, or goes in a different direction

Materials

● student handouts (pages 23–27)

● plastic tarp

● eggs

● stopwatch

● materials to build parachute (brought in by students; some common materials used have been plastic garbage bags, string, fishing line, bubble wrap, cotton balls, milk cartons, Styrofoam cups, egg cartons, old umbrellas, straws, balloons [no helium], handkerchiefs, and strawberry baskets)

Time Frame

Two class periods to design and construct the parachutes, plus 1 class period for the actual Egg-Drop Day

(continued)

Great Parachute Egg Drop

(continued)

Getting Started

Bring in an egg and show it to students. Ask: *What do you think will happen if I drop this egg?* (*It will break.*) *What could slow down its descent and keep it from breaking?* Challenge students to design and construct parachutes and egg holders that will keep an egg intact when dropped from a height of at least 16 feet (about 5 meters). Review some of the physics concepts students should keep in mind when building their parachute, such as gravity, air resistance, acceleration, and more.

Pair up students and distribute copies of the student handout. Allow students a couple of days to design and construct their parachutes in class. We like to increase the competition by awarding a prize for the longest "hang time" that safely carries the egg to the ground.

On Egg-Drop Day, bring in the eggs and cover the ground with a large plastic tarp. (We always make students responsible for cleaning up their own mess.) Bring a stopwatch to time each parachute's descent. Have students record their own time, as they will later use this to calculate the speed of each parachute's descent. Instruct students to take notes on the other parachutes as well.

When everyone's parachutes have been tested, have students write a report, "eggs-plaining" how their design worked to coun-teract the forces that normally act to break a dropped egg. The report should include a labeled picture of their parachute design.

◆ ◆ ◆ ◆ ◆ ◆ ◆ **Tips** ◆ ◆ ◆ ◆ ◆ ◆ ◆

- The clearer your grading rubric, the better students understand your expectations. Provide them with a clear idea of how you will assess them.

- We've included a writing frame for the project, which is great for English language learners!

- Videotape the egg-drop event to show to students the following year. Seeing video footage of previous egg-drop events helps students create better designs.

---

15 Standards-Based Science Activities Kids Will Love! • Scholastic Teaching Resources

Name: _____   Date: _____

Great Parachute Egg Drop

■ ■

Project Goal

Design a parachute that can carry an egg safely to the ground. Your goal is to have the slowest time and the safest landing, leaving your egg intact.

To Do

❶ Plan your parachute and egg holder. What materials will you use? How will you construct the parachute and holder?

❷ You will have one class day to build your parachute. Bring your materials on _____. The Egg-Drop Day will be on _____.

❸ After the Egg-Drop Day, write a report that details your egg's flight and includes the following physics vocabulary. (You must use the vocabulary correctly in the context of your egg's journey.)

✔ Gravity   ✔ Momentum

✔ Air resistance   ✔ Speed

✔ Acceleration   ✔ Friction

✔ Kinetic energy   ✔ Balanced, unbalanced forces

✔ Potential energy

Set up your report in the following manner:

Paragraph 1: Describe your egg's flight and your parachute's construction. What materials did you use? Did your chute open immediately? Provide a labeled picture of your parachute.

Paragraph 2: Using the physics vocabulary above (underline each time you use one of the words), describe the physics behind the egg's flight.

Paragraph 3: Which parachute worked best and why? Describe the best time's parachute and construction, and why you think it worked best!

Due date: _____

Name: _____ Date: _____

Great Parachute Egg Drop Data Sheet

Team	Distance (meters)	Time (seconds)	Speed (m/sec)	Egg Broken (Y/N)	Comments About Design

After the Egg Drop:

1. Calculate the speed of each drop. (speed = distance/time)

2. Put an "F" next to the fastest drop.

3. Put an "S" next to the slowest drop.

4. Answer the questions on the next page.

Due date: _____   *15 Standards-Based Science Activities Kids Will Love!* • Scholastic Teaching Resources

Name: _____ Date: _____

Great Parachute Egg Drop QUESTIONS

■ ■

1. What things affected the rate of descent (e.g., material, size, weight)?

_____

_____

2. Describe the parachute that descended the fastest. What do you think made it descend so fast?

_____

_____

_____

3. Describe the parachute that descended the slowest. What do you think made it descend so slow?

_____

_____

_____

4. What type of container worked best for the egg drop? Why?

_____

_____

5. What type of padding worked best for the egg drop? Why?

_____

_____

6. What type of chute material worked best for the egg drop? Why?

_____

_____

7. How would you modify or change your parachute to improve its performance?

_____

_____

_____

15 Standards-Based Science Activities Kids Will Love! • Scholastic Teaching Resources   **Due date:** _____

Name: _____ Date: _____

Great Parachute Egg Drop WRITING FRAME

■ ■

Paragraph 1: Introduction (*What will you tell the reader in the upcoming paragraphs; for example, details about the flight, forces of physics, the best parachute design?*)
This report is about the flight of my parachute.

_____

_____

Paragraph 2 detail: (*What will paragraph 2 be about?*)

_____

_____

Paragraph 3 detail: (*What will paragraph 3 be about?*)

_____

_____

Paragraph 2: (*Description of your egg's flight*)
Topic sentence: Our/My parachute's flight was successful/unsuccessful because …

_____

Detail 1: (*Direction of the flight*)
The parachute dropped straight down / with a slanted descent/…

_____

Detail 2: (*How the parachute operated*)
The parachute opened immediately/partially opened/…

_____

Detail 3: (*The effect the parachute had on the egg's flight*)
The parachute slowed it down/put it out of balance/…

_____

Detail 4: (*The egg's speed/how the container landed*)
The parachute landed quickly/ softly/ with a thud/…

_____

(continued)

Due date: _____   *15 Standards-Based Science Activities Kids Will Love!* • Scholastic Teaching Resources

Great Parachute Egg Drop WRITING FRAME

(continued)

■ ■

Paragraph 3: (*Explain the physics concepts behind your egg's flight*)
Topic sentence: Our parachute had to overcome many forces during its flight …

_____

_____

Detail 1: (*gravity*)
The force of gravity acted on my parachute by …

_____

Detail 2: (*air resistance*)
Air resistance played a role by …

_____

Detail 3: (*acceleration*)
During the parachute's descent, the acceleration …

_____

Detail 4: (*kinetic/potential energy*)
There was more kinetic energy during … and more potential energy during …

_____

Detail 5: (*speed*)
In order to determine the parachute's speed, we …

_____

Detail 6: (*friction*)
The force of friction affected the flight by …

_____

Detail 7: (*momentum*)
As the parachute headed downward, its momentum …

_____

Detail 8: (*balanced/unbalanced forces*)
As a great force acted upon the parachute, it …

_____

15 Standards-Based Science Activities Kids Will Love! • Scholastic Teaching Resources

Due date: _____

Name: _____

▪ ▪ ▪ ▪ ▪ ▪ ▪ ▪ Parachute Egg Drop ▪ ▪ ▪ ▪ ▪ ▪ ▪ ▪

Not Evident				Evident
0	**1**	**2**	**3**	**4**

0 1 2 3 4 1. Does the report consist of four well-developed paragraphs (introduction, two body paragraphs, and a conclusion paragraph)?

0 1 2 3 4 2. Does the introduction include details about the upcoming paragraphs in the report?

0 1 2 3 4 3. Does the topic sentence of each paragraph clearly state the main idea of that paragraph?

0 1 2 3 4 4. Are important details included to support the topic sentence of each paragraph?

0 1 2 3 4 5. Does the report include details about the egg's flight (for example, whether it was successful, the direction the flight took, the parachute's operation, the effects of the parachute on the egg's flight, and a description of its landing)?

0 1 2 3 4 6. Does the report include a detailed explanation of the physics involved in the egg's flight, using key physics vocabulary listed on the student handout?

0 1 2 3 4 7. Does the conclusion paragraph of the report include a clear justification of what you think would be the best parachute design as well as a summary of the main ideas in the report?

Points: _____/28

Planetary Adventure Travel Poster

Overview

Students will create a travel poster or a PowerPoint presentation (an "infomercial") of a brand-new vacation resort on a planet in the solar system or the planet's moon. Their presentation should take into consideration the features and characteristics of the planet or moon's natural resources. This project will result in many beautiful posters to display throughout your classroom.

Science Standards

✓ knows that the Earth is one of several planets that orbit the Sun and that the Moon orbits the Earth

✓ knows that astronomical objects in space are massive in size and are separated from one another by vast distances

✓ knows characteristics and movement patterns of the nine planets in our solar system (e.g., planets differ in size, composition, and surface features; some planets have moons, rings or particles, and other satellites orbiting them)

Materials

● student handout (page 31)

● large butcher paper/poster paper per group of 3–4 students

● markers

● scissors

● construction paper

● glue

● rulers

● planet fact sheets (We use the Internet, textbooks, CD-ROMs, and any other resources on planet.)

Time Frame

3 or 4 class periods for students to design and create the poster, plus 1 class period to make their oral presentations

(continued)

Planetary Adventure Travel Poster

(continued)

Getting Started

If possible, bring in some travel brochures or posters from different resorts and share them with students. Explain to students that they will be planning a resort for one of the planets or moons in our solar system.

Divide the class into eight groups and assign each group a planet (excluding Earth). Explain that their main goal is to develop housing, entertainment, food, and energy resources on their assigned planet (or a moon of that planet). Brainstorm with students some of the ways to incorporate the planet's features into their resort. For example, Jupiter's moon Io is volcanic so they could build a geothermal power plant to tap the moon's natural resources for energy. Remind students that they need to develop food and water resources because bringing them from Earth is not an option. Encourage students to conceive of various adventure trips using the planet or moon's natural features. For example, "Hike through the largest canyon in the solar system, Valles Marineris on Mars."

Distribute the student handout and discuss the requirements with students. When students finish their posters, invite them to give an oral presentation, explaining the features of their resort to the class.

> ◆ ◆ ◆ ◆ ◆ ◆ ◆ ◆ **Tips** ◆ ◆ ◆ ◆ ◆ ◆ ◆ ◆
>
> - Distribute travel brochures to each group so students can get a sense of design layout and see what resorts usually have to offer.
> - Advise students to divide the work requirements among themselves so that each student is working on a different aspect of the project.
> - The larger the paper students use for their posters, the better the result. This way, students have a lot of room for their explanations.

Name: _____ Date: _____

Planetary Adventure Travel Poster/Infomercial

■ ■

Project Goal
Imagine that you have just opened a brand-new vacation resort on your assigned planet. Your job is to create a poster or infomercial (using PowerPoint) to attract visitors to your planetary vacation spot. Be creative!

To Do

❶ Gather pertinent information about your planet, such as temperature, gravity, length of year, amount of sunlight, and distance from Earth. Use this information to create your poster or infomercial.

❷ Your poster or infomercial should include the following information:

✔ How will your visitors get to your planet? (Think about what modes of transportation are available, how far your planet is from Earth, and how long it currently takes to get there. A spaceship can travel 40,000 km/hr or 25,000 mi/hr. The speed of light is 300,000 km/hr.)

✔ What kind of climate/atmosphere should visitors expect when they stay at your planetary resort?

✔ What type of accommodations (housing or lodging) will be available for guests?

✔ Is there water available? If not, how will you get/make water for your guests?

✔ What is there for guests to eat?

✔ Where will you get energy from? (Take into consideration what can be transformed into energy either on the planet or one of its moons.)

✔ What type of entertainment or activities will you offer your clientele? (These should relate to the features of your planet or moon.)

✔ What other unique characteristics does your planet or its moon(s) have that would attract visitors?

❸ Give a presentation to the class about your planetary (or lunar) vacation resort. Pretend you are an advertising or marketing executive trying to attract new clients to your resort.

Due date: _____

Name: _____

▪ ▪ ▪ ▪ **Planetary Adventure Travel Poster** ▪ ▪ ▪ ▪

CRITERIA	SCORE
CONTENT Information is factual and shows evidence of careful research, describing the planet or moon's features and characteristics in detail. Design of the vacation resort/poster/infomercial takes into account and incorporates these features and characteristics, showing a thorough understanding of scientific concepts and their practical applications.	(_____/40 points)
CREATIVITY Poster or infomercial is colorful, attractive, and eye-catching. The name of the planet and resort is large and prominent. Illustrations and photographs are labeled or captioned with informative text.	(_____/30 points)
ORAL PRESENTATION Information about the planet or moon and the vacation resort is presented in a clear, loud voice for everyone to hear. Presenter(s) used the poster as a visual aid, pointing out different features of the planet/moon and vacation resort. Team members could answer questions regarding their project correctly and thoughtfully.	(_____/30 points)
TOTAL: _____/100 points	

Comments:

_____

_____

It's Our Environment Pamphlet

Overview

We assign this project as a wrap-up to our unit on global warming. Students create a pamphlet discussing the environment and human impact on our land, air, and water. They may cover any of the following topics: population, land usage, natural resources, recycling (waste management), and air and water pollution. You will love the products students create and the amount of knowledge they gain.

Science Standards

✓ knows that changes in the environment can have different effects on different organisms

✓ knows that all organisms (including humans) can cause changes in their environments, and these changes can be beneficial or detrimental

Materials

● student handout (page 34)

● large piece of construction paper per 3–4 students

● markers

● resources on environmental topics (We give students packets of information that we assemble from the Internet and pull all relevant library books.)

● magazines (students can cut out pictures to use in their pamphlets)

Time Frame

Two class periods to create the pamphlets and 1 class period to present them

Getting Started

List and review the various environmental issues you have discussed in class. Divide the class into groups of 3 or 4 students and distribute the student handout.

Explain to students that each group will create a pamphlet that discusses the environmental topic of their choice. The pamphlet should introduce and describe the issue, what has caused this issue to be a problem, what its effects are, and what people can do to help solve the problem. Encourage students to cut out pictures to illustrate their issue. At the back of the pamphlet, each student should write a biography paragraph that includes how he or she plans to help preserve our planet.

◆ ◆ ◆ ◆ ◆ ◆ Tips ◆ ◆ ◆ ◆ ◆ ◆

● Keep any great pamphlets for the following year. You'll find the better your samples are, the better your next products will be!

● Bring in pamphlets or brochures to give students ideas about design layout and organization.

● If possible, allot a day in the computer lab for students to word process their pamphlet. You could also assign the typing for homework.

Name: _____ **Date:** _____

Environmental Pamphlet

■ ■

Project Goal

Conduct research on an environmental issue and create a pamphlet that promotes social awareness and action in relation to this environmental issue.

To Do

❶ Fold a sheet of construction paper into three panels, like a pamphlet or brochure. On the front panel, write a catchy title that tells readers what the brochure will be about.

❷ The finished pamphlet should contain the following information:

✔ a description of the environmental issue

✔ what caused this issue to become a problem

✔ what are some of its effects

✔ what people can do to help resolve the problem

✔ a biography of each student in the group, including what he or she personally plans to do to help preserve the environment

Due date: _____   *15 Standards-Based Science Activities Kids Will Love!* • Scholastic Teaching Resources

Name: _____

■ ■ ■ ■ ■ ■ **Environmental Pamphlet** ■ ■ ■ ■ ■ ■

CRITERIA	SCORE
PRESENTATION Pamphlet is neat, colorful, and attractive. Photos and/or illustrations are properly captioned and support the content. Text is legible, preferably typewritten, and has been proofread for spelling and grammar.	(_____/40 points)
CONTENT Contains all the required information listed on the student page. Factual and detailed information shows evidence of careful research and planning. Shows a thorough understanding of the specific environmental issue, its causes and effects, and how people can help resolve the issue. Content is organized in a logical way.	(_____/40 points)
BIOGRAPHY Contains basic information about each member of the team, as well as realistic and practical plans for helping preserve the planet.	(_____/20 points)
TOTAL: _____/100 points	

Comments:

_____

_____

_____

_____

Elements of the Planet Rolyat

We chose to use fire and water as symbols because they are opposite to each other and react differently. This will give a clear way to distinguish between elements. To make the table easier to read, we put the water on the top and the fire on the bottom. We assigned each element a symbol by their hardness, reaction with water, and melting points. The hardness of an element has a relationship to the reaction of water. Both also have a relationship to the melting point. If an element has a water symbol, then it is hard, doesn't react with water, and has a high temperature melting point. The elements with a fire symbol have the direct opposite characteristics of water symbols. They are soft, react with water, and have a low temperature melting point. We put the water and fire symbols elements left to right by their increasing mass.

Overview

This assignment allows students to simulate the process scientist Dmitri Mendeleev went through in designing the periodic table of elements. Students act as scientists and decide how to organize elements into a useful table or chart based on various characteristics.

Science Standards _____

✓ knows that substances can be classified by their physical and chemical properties

✓ knows that matter is made up of tiny particles called atoms, and different arrangements of atoms into groups compose all substances

✓ knows that substances containing only one kind of atom are elements and do not break down by normal laboratory reactions; over 100 different elements exist

✓ knows that many elements can be grouped according to similar properties

Materials

● student handout (pages 38–39)

● index cards

● construction paper

● markers

● glue

● scissors

● poster of periodic table of elements (or make copies to pass out to students)

Time Frame

2 or 3 class periods

Getting Started

Display a poster of the periodic table of elements (or pass out copies to students). Ask students: *How are the elements arranged in this table?* (*They are arranged in order of increasing atomic weight and according to similarity in properties.*) Explain that scientist Dmitri Mendeleev looked for patterns in and studied characteristics of elements to help him develop the periodic table.

Next, inform students about a newly discovered planet, called the planet Rolyat. (You can rename the planet if you wish—our planet is the name of our school, Taylor, spelled backward.) Scientists have identified 10 mystery elements on this planet. Tell students that they will work in pairs to design a periodic table of elements—a creative system of organization based on the elements' properties. Distribute the student handout, which contains a chart of the 10 mystery elements and their characteristics.

(continued)

Elements of the Planet Rolyat

(continued)

Direct students to create a rough draft of their table and share it with you before moving on to the final project. Distribute 10 index cards to each pair of students. Have them use the index cards to create "element boxes," which will include all the known information about each element, including a name that students think up themselves. Encourage students to name each element based on a theme; for example, after favorite sports players. Challenge students to look for patterns in the element boxes and come up with a way to organize them that makes sense.

Explain to students that there will be two parts to their final grade on this project. The majority of their grade will come from the periodic table's level of organization. The more sophisticated the organization, the higher their grade. (There can be at least three patterns incorporated into one table.) Points will also be rewarded for creativity. For example, one pair of students noticed a pattern relating to hardness and divided their elements into a hard and soft group. They made their table into the shape of an egg. The soft elements were arranged on the inside of the egg and the hard elements made up the eggshell. Students must include a key to reading their "element boxes." They should also label or draw arrows on their final table to clearly illustrate the patterns of organization.

◆ ◆ ◆ ◆ ◆ ◆ ◆ ◆ **Tips** ◆ ◆ ◆ ◆ ◆ ◆ ◆ ◆

- Students can sometimes get caught up in the creative side of the project. Emphasize that you are looking for patterns of organization in their charts.

- We encourage students to compete for the best table in the class. Explain that the winning project will be displayed as the official table for the planet Rolyat.

Name: _____   Date: _____

Elements of the Planet Rolyat

■ ■

Project Goal

Design a periodic table that organizes the 10 mystery elements listed below into a useful chart. Consider how scientist Dmitri Mendeleev looked for patterns in elements and studied their characteristics to design the periodic table of elements.

Background

A space probe recently returned from a mission to the planet Rolyat. While the probe was on the planet surface, highly sophisticated scientific equipment detected the presence of 10 previously unknown elements. Luckily, rock and soil samples collected by the probe's robotic arms contain small samples of these elements, and chemists have been able to test each of the elements in the lab. They have found out that the elements have the following properties:

Element	Mass	Color	Hardness	Melting point (Celsius)	Reacts with water
A	5	turquoise	hard	1050°	no
B	3	silvery black	soft	−300°	yes
C	1	yellow	hard	1000°	no
D	7	gray	soft	400°	yes
E	10	pink	hard	1200°	no
F	15	silvery black	soft	−100°	yes
G	9	silvery black	soft	−200°	yes
H	14	black	soft	300°	yes
I	2	turquoise	hard	900°	no
J	6	tan	hard	1000°	no

(continued)

Due date: _____

15 Standards-Based Science Activities Kids Will Love! • Scholastic Teaching Resources

Name: _____ Date: _____

Elements of the Planet Rolyat

(continued)

■ ▪ ■ ▪ ▪ ▪ ■ ▪ ■ ▪ ▪ ■ ▪ ▪ ■ ▪ ■ ▪ ■ ▪ ▪ ▪ ▪ ■ ▪ ▪ ■ ▪ ■

To Do

❶ Your job is to work with a fellow scientist to design a periodic table of elements for the planet Rolyat. Experts will pick the best table as the official periodic table of elements for the planet Rolyat.

❷ Name each of the 10 elements found on Rolyat and come up with a symbol for each element.

❸ Decide how to set up an "element box" that will clearly show all the important information or properties about each element (mass, color, hardness, melting point, reactivity with water). Use an index card for each of your element boxes. Remember, your element boxes must be easy to read and understand.

❹ Design a key for your box.

❺ Group the elements based on their properties. Organize the 10 boxes into a chart based on the elements' properties.

❻ After your rough draft is complete, transfer your table to construction paper and decorate.

Helpful Hint:

Remember that experts will be judging your periodic table based on how easy it is to read and understand, as well as how attractive it is and how cleverly it is organized.

Due date: _____

Name: _____

■ ■ ■ ■ ■ # Elements of the Planet Rolyat ■ ■ ■ ■ ■

CRITERIA	SCORE
1. Identified similarities and differences in properties of the elements	(_____/20)
2. Identified properties useful for sorting	(_____/20)
3. Classified elements by their properties into at least two groups	(_____/20)
4. Defined the criteria and rationale for organizing the elements	(_____/20)
5. Designed a creative table or chart to organize the elements	(_____/20)
TOTAL: _____/100 points	

Comments:

_____

_____

✂ ---

Grading Rubric ## Elements of the Planet Rolyat

Name: _____

CRITERIA	SCORE
1. Identified similarities and differences in properties of the elements	(_____/20)
2. Identified properties useful for sorting	(_____/20)
3. Classified elements by their properties into at least two groups	(_____/20)
4. Defined the criteria and rationale for organizing the elements	(_____/20)
5. Designed a creative table or chart to organize the elements	(_____/20)
TOTAL: _____/100 points	

Comments:

_____

_____

From a Molecule's Point of View

Overview

Students will create a cartoon describing a water molecule as it goes through a series of phase changes. This activity can be used as an assignment or as a unit assessment on matter.

Science Standards

✓ knows that matter has different states (i.e., solid, liquid, gas) and that each state has distinct physical properties; some common materials such as water can be changed from one state to another by heating or cooling

✓ knows that matter is made up of tiny particles called atoms, and different arrangements of atoms into groups compose all substances

✓ knows that atoms often combine to form a molecule, the smallest particle of a substance that retains its properties

✓ knows that states of matter depend on molecular arrangement and motion (e.g., molecules in solids are packed tightly together and their movement is restricted to vibrations; molecules in liquids are loosely packed and move easily past each other; molecules in gases are quite far apart and move about freely)

Materials

◉ student handout (page 42)

◉ white construction paper

◉ crayons

◉ markers

◉ color pencils

Time Frame

One class period

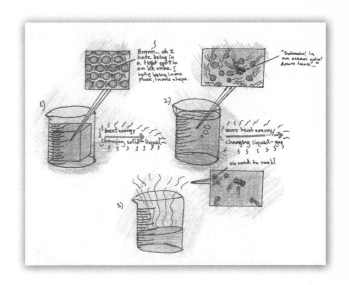

Getting Started

Ask students: *What are the three phases of matter?* (*Solid, liquid, and gas*) Review with students how each phase is different from the others.

Distribute the student handout and a sheet of white paper to each student. Explain to students that they will be creating a cartoon describing a water molecule as it goes through the different phases of matter. Students should include particle arrangement, molecular movements, shape, volume, and energy changes in their cartoon. Have students write in the first person, from the molecule's point of view. Encourage students to be creative and to use their imagination.

◆◆◆◆◆◆◆◆◆ **Tip** ◆◆◆◆◆◆◆◆◆

◉ Make sure that students represent all three of the common phases of matter—solid, liquid, and gas. Explain that it doesn't matter in what phase the molecule starts and in what phase it ends as long as the molecule changes between all three phases.

Name: _____   Date: _____

From a Molecule's Point of View

■ ■

Project Goal

Create a cartoon about a water molecule going through a series of phase changes. Pretend that you are the molecule, and write the cartoon in the first person.

To Do

❶ Imagine that you are a water molecule who is going through a series of phase changes. Write a story to describe your experiences as you change. You can either be:
- a molecule of ice changing to liquid water then to water vapor; or
- a molecule of water vapor changing to liquid water and then to ice.

❷ Be specific, making sure to include particle arrangements, molecular movements, energy changes, and shape/volume properties. Be creative and use your imagination. Write in the first person, as if the molecule were talking.

Example:

Hi, my name is Bob the water molecule. I'm going to tell you about a fascinating adventure that I had today. I started out by clinging to a cold bottle of water. (How I got there is a whole other story.) Anyway, I'm hanging around with some other molecules but we had enough space to comfortably slide around each other. In fact, I started to move so much that I slid right off the bottle and hit the ground with a splat. Wow, that hurt! However, it was such a beautiful day with the sun shining that I wasn't too upset. While I was sitting there I noticed that I was getting hotter. I also felt like I had more energy than I did earlier. I started to feel different, like my body was changing. Is this what puberty feels like? I suddenly realized that I was changing into a gas...

❸ Illustrate the story you have just created. You may want to divide your paper to create a three-panel cartoon, illustrating each phase change.

Due date: _____   *15 Standards-Based Science Activities Kids Will Love!* • Scholastic Teaching Resources

Name: _____

▪ ▪ ▪ ▪ From a Molecule's Point of View ▪ ▪ ▪ ▪

CRITERIA	SCORE	COMMENTS
1. Are all three phases of matter represented in the story/cartoon?	(_____/5 points)	
2. Does the story/cartoon describe in detail each phase of matter?	(_____/30 points)	
3. Does the story/cartoon describe in detail the changes that occur during each phase change?	(_____/30 points)	
4. Is the story imaginative and engaging?	(_____/20 points)	
5. Are the illustrations neat, colorful, and attractive?	(_____/15 points)	
TOTAL: _____/100 points		

Science Superstar on Video

Overview

We use this as a unit assessment tool, where students demonstrate their expertise on one topic from our physics unit. (Of course, you can use this with any of your science units.) Students develop a presentation in the style of *Bill Nye the Science Guy*. They may choose to do a skit, an experimental demonstration, or perform a music video.

Science Standards

✓ understands the nature of scientific knowledge

✓ understands the nature of scientific inquiry

✓ understands the scientific enterprise

Materials

- student handouts (pages 45–46)
- poster board
- lab equipment (will vary depending on what students will want to use for their presentation)
- video camera and blank videotapes, if possible

Time Frame

One class period for students to work and organize their presentations, plus 1 or 2 class periods to present. The majority of students' prep work should be done outside of class.

Getting Started

If possible, show a couple of *Bill Nye* videos to give students an idea of what a science skit might look like.

Divide the class into groups of 3 or 4 students, and distribute the student handout. Assign each group a science concept for their topic, such as friction, gravity, or motion. (We divided our physics unit into nine concepts and asked a representative from each group to pick a topic out of a hat. We then gave the groups an opportunity to exchange topics with one another if they choose to do so.)

If you have the necessary video equipment, consider letting students videotape their presentations and show their videos on TV. Another option is to have students perform live in front of the class. Each presentation must include a complete and thorough description of the science concept and the theories involved. Students should include a visual representation of the topic, such as charts, graphs, or diagrams, drawn on poster board. Vocabulary and examples must be accurate.

Encourage students to be original, clever, and amusing. They can rewrite current songs with appropriate science lyrics, wear costumes, and be as creative as possible.

◆ ◆ ◆ ◆ ◆ ◆ ◆ ◆ **Tip** ◆ ◆ ◆ ◆ ◆ ◆ ◆ ◆

- Help pace English language learners by giving them due dates for creating a rough-draft storyboard of their ideas. Assign a number of scenes for each date.

Name: _____ **Date:** _____

Science Superstar Video

■ ▪ ■ ▪ ■ ▪ ■ ▪ ■ ▪ ■ ▪ ■ ▪ ■ ▪ ■ ▪ ■ ▪ ■ ▪ ■ ▪ ■ ▪ ■ ▪ ■ ▪ ■ ▪ ■ ▪ ■

Project Goal
Demonstrate your expertise on a topic from our science unit by performing a science skit in a *Bill Nye*–style video. Your skit should include key concepts and vocabulary, and show at least one experiment or demonstration. You may also perform a music video with updated lyrics from your science topic.

To Do

❶ Use the planner (from your teacher) to decide what to include in your "show."

❷ You will perform OR show your videotape on _____. Your presentation should include:

✔ a complete and thorough introduction of your topic. What are the theories involved? Are there formulas? Why is this useful to know for everyday life? Describe any labs or activities we did in class.

✔ science vocabulary that is used correctly

✔ a visual representation of your topic, either by doing a demonstration or an experiment, or by providing some other visual aid

Make your presentation as original, creative, and entertaining as possible. You may rewrite songs with appropriate science lyrics, wear costumes, and let your imagination run wild.

15 Standards-Based Science Activities Kids Will Love! • Scholastic Teaching Resources

Due date: _____

Name: _____ Date: _____

Science Superstar PLANNER

■ ■

Use this outline to help you plan your project:

A. Topic Introduction

1. **Theories/Concepts:** What theories or concepts are associated with this topic? (Example: *A force is a push or pull on an object. It can cause things to be balanced or unbalanced. A balanced force is...*)

2. **Formulas:** What formulas go along with the concept?

3. **Key Vocabulary:** What words does the audience need to know and understand in relation to this topic?

4. **Labs/Activities:** What lab/activity did we do in class to show...?

B. Creative Ways to Present the Information

1. Do we have a great lead? How will we grab our audience?

2. How will we transition between scenes?

3. Who will narrate each scene?

4. How will we make each scene interesting and amusing?

5. How is this science concept useful in everyday life? What examples can we provide?

C. Demonstrations/Visuals/Experiments

1. How will we show the audience what the concepts are? What activities or labs can we do?

2. What charts, graphs, posters, flowcharts, pictures, or diagrams can we use to give the audience a better picture of what we are talking about?

Due date: _____

15 Standards-Based Science Activities Kids Will Love! • Scholastic Teaching Resources

Name: _____

▪ ▪ ▪ ▪ ▪ ▪ ▪ ▪ Science Superstar ▪ ▪ ▪ ▪ ▪ ▪ ▪ ▪

CRITERIA	SCORE
Introduction and Mastery of Content ⦿ The presentation includes relevant theories and formulas and uses science vocabulary correctly. ⦿ The presentation includes a review of at least one lab or class activity. ⦿ The presentation explains how the concept is important to everyday life.	(_____/40 points)
Demonstrations/Visuals/Experiments ⦿ The presentation includes at least one demonstration or experiment. ⦿ The presentation includes at least one visual aid, such as a chart, graph, poster, flowchart, picture, or diagram.	(_____/30 points)
Creativity and Preparedness ⦿ The presenters were prepared and used clear, loud voices when sharing information. ⦿ The presentation was creative and amusing, while covering the necessary key concepts.	(_____/30 points)
TOTAL: _____/100 points	

Comments:

_____

_____

_____

_____

Mystery of the Meddling Monkey

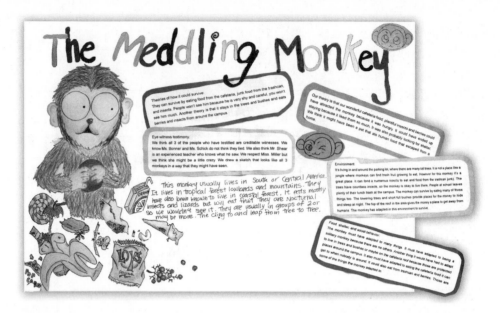

Overview

This is a fun project that requires students to utilize their critical-thinking skills and argue for or against a probable sighting of an unidentified animal. You will need help from other teachers (or other credible adults), who will report a sighting of what they believe to be a monkey among the trees near the school. Students must develop a theory about the monkey's existence (or nonexistence) and support it with evidence. They learn how to utilize supporting testimony and eliminate unlikely evidence. We have used this project as an assessment at the end of our adaptation unit.

Science Standards _____

✓ knows that an organism's patterns of behavior are related to the nature of that organism's environment (e.g., physical characteristics of the environment, availability of food and resources)

✓ knows factors that affect the number and types of organisms an ecosystem can support (e.g., available resources)

✓ knows basic ideas related to biological evolution

Materials

● student handout (page 50)

● *The Beast of Loch Ness* video (optional)

● eyewitnesses (invite other teachers to your class, or write their testimonies to read to students)

● sketches of monkeys (the Internet is a great source)

● resources on monkeys and your local environment

● large construction paper (for each group)

● markers

Time Frame

Three class periods, plus one class period to view the video, if available

(continued)

Mystery of the Meddling Monkey

(continued)

Getting Started

If possible, show the NOVA video *The Beast of Loch Ness*, which details evidence of the monster's existence and presents arguments as to why it couldn't really exist. The video will take up one class period. If you can't access the video, visit its companion Web site at http://www.pbs.org/wgbh/nova/lochness/.

Invite a few teachers to come to your class and give eyewitness testimony about a "monkey" they've seen among the trees near the school. (If teachers can't come, you can read aloud their "testimonies" to students instead. Adapt teachers' names and statements if you wish.) Show sketches of some monkeys to go with the teachers' accounts. (We tell students that professional sketch artists were brought in to draw what the eyewitnesses had seen.) The testimonies are fun for students because they know the teachers involved.

Divide the class into groups of four students. You may want to assign which groups are arguing for or against the monkey's existence. Distribute copies of the student handout and the monkey sketches to each group. Read over the directions with students and emphasize that they will need to provide information about the environment (e.g., food, shelter, and other resources in the area) in order to argue one way or another. Go over the eyewitness testimonies and the monkey sketches. If possible, provide students with resources on the habitat in which you live. For example, we give our students information on California habitats. If you have access to a computer lab, students can use the Internet to look up the information themselves. Students should then gather the evidence they need to develop their theory. When students have finished their research, distribute construction paper and markers for students to create their presentations.

◆ ◆ ◆ ◆ ◆ ◆ ◆ **Tips** ◆ ◆ ◆ ◆ ◆ ◆ ◆

- Have students present their cases in front of the class as sort of a convention on the sightings.
- Using real teachers as eyewitnesses makes the project more believable to students.

Name: _____ Date: _____

Mystery of the Meddling Monkey

■ ■

Project Goal

Read or listen to eyewitness accounts of a mysterious monkey that has been sighted around the school. Then conduct research and present evidence that proves or disproves the monkey's presence in the area.

To Do

❶ As you listen to eyewitness accounts, take notes on important information such as what the monkey looked like, what it was doing, and where it was seen.

❷ Conduct research on both the monkey and your immediate environment. Consider: What does the monkey need to survive? Can the environment support its needs?

❸ Create a poster to present your evidence. Your poster should include the following:

✔ A colorful, realistic picture of the animal that was seen

✔ 5 details about the environment (e.g., vegetation, water source, shelter, and so on) that either support or don't support the existence of a monkey

✔ 3 supporting paragraphs of evidence for your argument—in other words, your interpretation of how this environment could or could not support a monkey

✔ Your theory: As scientists, offer a theory of what might have happened that supports your case.

❹ Present your case to the class, using your poster as a visual aid.

Name: _____

▪ ▪ ▪ Mystery of the Meddling Monkey ▪ ▪ ▪

Score   Poster _____

3   Drawing of monkey is realistic and very detailed. The background shows the monkey in its environment, which is also realistic and colorful. Overall, the poster is very neat and attractive.

2   Drawing of monkey is somewhat realistic and includes some details. There is a bit of a background. The poster is neat and attractive.

1   Drawing of monkey is very sketchy and includes no details. There is no background. It doesn't appear like much effort was put into making the poster look attractive.

Score   Research and Evidence _____

3   Team presented five or more details about the environment (e.g., shelter, access to food and water, etc.) to support their case as to whether or not a monkey could exist in that environment.

2   Team presented three or four details about the environment to support their case as to whether or not a monkey could exist in that environment.

1   Team presented only up to two details about the environment to support their case as to whether or not a monkey could exist in that environment.

Score   Theory _____

3   Used appropriate information and prior knowledge to develop a theory on the monkey's presence. The team's interpretation of the facts was logical, and they used sound reasoning to defend their case.

2   Used information to develop a theory on the monkey's presence. Their interpretation of the information was generally sound, but did not always clearly support their argument.

1   Used mostly conjecture (guesses) to develop a theory on the monkey's presence. Reasoning was not very clear and logical.

Total Score: _____/9

Comments:

_____

_____

_____

Biomes and Endangered Species Report

Overview

Students will work in groups to research and present information on one of the world's major biomes through either a written report or a HyperStudio multimedia presentation.

Science Standards

✓ knows that an organism's patterns of behavior are related to the nature of that organism's environment

✓ knows that changes in the environment can have different effects on different organisms

✓ knows that all organisms (including humans) cause changes in their environments, and these changes can be beneficial or detrimental

✓ knows that all individuals of a species that exist together at a given place and time make up a population, and all populations living together and the physical factors with which they interact compose an ecosystem

✓ knows factors that affect the number and types of organisms an ecosystem can support

✓ knows ways in which organisms interact and depend on one another through food chains and food webs in an ecosystem

Materials

⦿ student handout (pages 53–54)

⦿ resources on biomes and endangered species

⦿ Hyperstudio software (optional)

⦿ access to a computer or computer lab

⦿ construction paper

⦿ markers

Time Frame

About 3 to 5 class periods to do the research and complete the finished product

Getting Started

Ask students: *What is a biome?* (*A major ecological community that includes all plants, animals, and other organisms that live in it*) *What are some of the biomes we have on Earth?* (*Tundra, coniferous forest, deciduous forest, grassland, tropical rain forest, desert, ocean, wetlands, and fresh water*)

Divide the class into groups of four, and distribute the handout to students. Inform them that each group will be given a different biome to study. Each group will become the biome "experts" and present a report on their assigned biome. In addition, they will report on an endangered species that lives in that particular biome and include information such as how it became endangered and what can be done to save it from extinction. Give students the option of presenting their reports in either a written/oral form or as a Hyperstudio multimedia presentation.

Name: _____   Date: _____

Biomes and Endangered Species Report

■ ■

Project Goal

Conduct research and report on one of the world's major biomes as well as an endangered species that lives there. Your presentation could be in the form of a written and oral report or a Hyperstudio multimedia presentation.

To Do

❶ Use the Internet and other resources to conduct research on your biome and on an endangered species that lives in it. Make sure to look for the following information:

✔ The general features and conditions of the biome. Where would you find your biome (specific countries or regions)? What are some of the major abiotic factors that affect life in this habitat (e.g., rainfall, temperature ranges, light intensity, soil type)?

✔ At least three types of plant life that are typical of or common in this biome. How have these plants adapted to the conditions of the biome?

✔ At least three types of animal life that are typical of or common in this biome. How have these animals adapted to the conditions of the biome?

✔ Information about an endangered species living in the biome. What are the common and scientific names of your species? What does it look like (e.g., size, color, weight)? What does it eat and how does it get its food? Who are its natural predators? What is threatening the species (e.g., habitat loss, pollution, hunting, competition from new species, capture for zoos, incidental kills)? Approximately how many such species are left in the world? What contribution does your species make to the world (e.g., economic, ecological, medicinal, or even aesthetic)? How is your species being helped or protected from extinction? In your opinion, what is the best solution to help protect your species further?

❷ Decide whether you want to write a report or create a Hyperstudio multimedia presentation. If you decide to go with a written report, you can choose to present it as a mini-book, magazine, or pop-up book. Divide your report into four sections according to the information above. See next page if you are using Hyperstudio to create your report.

(continued)

15 Standards-Based Science Activities Kids Will Love! • Scholastic Teaching Resources   **Due date:** _____

Name: _____ Date: _____

Biomes & Endangered Species Report
(continued)

■ ■

Hyperstudio Multimedia Presentation:

This is a great alternative if you are familiar with Hyperstudio. Each group member should create a Hyperstudio stack on one of the four points listed above (i.e., abiotic factors, animals, plants, or endangered species). Your presentation should include the following elements:

✔ a title card with the name of your biome and links to each group member's Hyperstudio stack

✔ each group member's Hyperstudio stack—each stack should include information relating to your topic, pictures, an Internet link, and a button linking your stack to the title card

✔ a high level of detail and creativity

Due date: _____

Name: _____

▪ ▪ ▪ Biomes and Endangered Species Report ▪ ▪ ▪

WRITTEN REPORT	SCORE
• Does your report include general information as well as details about the biome (e.g., where it can be found, what factors/conditions of the biome affect life in this habitat)?	_____/10
• Does it list up to three types of plants that live in the biome?	_____/10
• Does it list up to three types of animals that live in the biome?	_____/10
• Does it explain how these life-forms have adapted to conditions of the biome?	_____/10
• Does it talk about an endangered species that lives in this biome?	_____/10
• Does it include relevant information about the endangered species, such as its name, what it looks like, what it eats and how it gets its food, why it is endangered, and so on?	_____/10
• Does it discuss how this endangered species is being protected from extinction?	_____/10
• Does your report include your opinion about how best to protect this species and its environment?	_____/10
• Is your report typed neatly?	_____/10
• Are important vocabulary words used and spelled correctly?	_____/10
TOTAL: _____/100 points	

HYPERSTUDIO PRESENTATION	SCORE
• Does your title card show the name of your biome and include working links to each group member's stack?	_____/10
• Is there a stack that describes the biome in detail?	_____/20*
• Is there a stack that lists up to three types of plants that live in the biome and how they have adapted to conditions in the biome?	_____/20*
• Is there a stack that lists up to three types of animals that live in the biome and how they have adapted to conditions in the biome?	_____/20*
• Is there a stack that reports on an endangered species that lives in that biome, including information about why it is endangered and what can be done to save it from extinction?	_____/20*
• Does the entire presentation show evidence of teamwork and creativity?	_____/10
TOTAL: _____/100 points	

* Make sure each stack includes detailed information about the topic, as well as relevant pictures, an Internet link, and a button that links back to the title card.

Public Service Announcement

Overview

Students develop a public service announcement about various important science topics affecting society, such as the environment, natural disasters, or health issues.

Science Standards

✓ understands the nature of scientific knowledge

✓ understands the scientific enterprise

Materials

- student handout (page 57)
- video camera and blank tapes, if possible
- butcher paper for background
- references on various science topics
- access to the Internet (for research)
- markers
- construction paper
- scissors
- glue

Time Frame

2 or 3 class periods for students to prepare and organize their materials and write their script, plus 1 or 2 class periods for students to present their public service announcements

Getting Started

Decide on the topic(s) you want students to cover and gather some reference materials for them. We usually look online for simple, easy explanations of the topic or use science textbooks.

Inform students that they will be creating a public service announcement about an important science issue that affects society. Each group's announcement will be video-taped and shown to the class.

Divide the class into groups of 3 or 4 students, and distribute the student handout. On a large piece of butcher paper (about 3 by 5 feet, depending on your supply), have each group create a backdrop that represents their topic; for example, if their topic is California habitats, they might draw a particular habitat and its native plants and animals, and write the name of the habitat. Students should also write a script that includes an introduction to the topic, problems or issues around the topic, and possible solutions or suggestions as to how people can help. Each student in the group should be responsible for one portion of the script and presentation.

◆ ◆ ◆ ◆ ◆ ◆ ◆ ◆ **Tips** ◆ ◆ ◆ ◆ ◆ ◆ ◆ ◆

- Tape some real public service announcements for students to watch in class so they can become familiar with the format.
- To ensure that everyone in the group contributes to the project, you may want to assign a portion to individual students.
- Remind students to pace themselves as they work on the background and script so they don't spend too much time on one part at the expense of the other.
- If you don't have access to video equipment, have students perform their public service announcements live in front of the class.

Name: _____ Date: _____

Public Service Announcement

▪ ▪

Project Goal

Write and perform a public service announcement about a particular science topic that affects society. This project will include a backdrop and a script, and your public service announcement will be videotaped or performed live in front of the class.

To Do

❶ Together with your team, develop a script regarding your topic. Include the following:

✔ Greeting or welcome (e.g., "Good morning! I am your host [your name] and today we will talk about...")

✔ Problems or issues about the topic

✔ Why these problems concern you (the viewers)

✔ Possible solutions

✔ How you (the viewers) can help

❷ Using a large piece of butcher paper, markers, and other art materials, create a backdrop that represents your topic.

❸ Decide who on your team will make the public service announcement on video. It could be just one person or the whole team.

15 Standards-Based Science Activities Kids Will Love! • Scholastic Teaching Resources

Due date: _____

Name: _____

▪ ▪ ▪ ▪ Public Service Announcement ▪ ▪ ▪ ▪

CRITERIA	SCORE
WRITTEN SCRIPT Introduces the science topic and discusses how it affects society. Explains any problems or issues related to the topic and how and why they concern us. Suggests possible solutions and what people can do to help.	(_____/20 points)
ORAL PRESENTATION Engages the audience and is presented in a lively manner. Information is expressed in a clear, loud voice that everyone could hear.	(_____/20 points)
BACKDROP AND PROPS Represent and support the topic in discussion. The backdrop is colorful and pleasing to the eye, and the props aid in further understanding of the topic.	(_____/10 points)

TOTAL: _____/50 points

Comments:

_____

_____

_____

_____

_____

The ABC's of Science: A Year in Review

The 8ᵗʰ Grade
ABC Book:
Beginning From A–Z

Marty Kwan
5/8/03
6ᵗʰ Science, Fiore

Overview

We tweaked this idea from our colleague Lori Musso's *25 Terrific Literature Activities for Readers of All Learning Styles* (Scholastic, 1999). She is a friend and colleague whom we admire greatly. Instead of a portfolio, this activity serves as our end-of-the-year wrap-up. Students review the science concepts we learned throughout the year and create a beautiful product in the process.

Science Standards _____

✓ understands the nature of scientific knowledge

✓ understands the nature of scientific inquiry

✓ understands the scientific enterprise

Materials

● student handout (page 60)

● portfolio of student work from the year

● construction paper

Time Frame

About a week (Students do most of the work outside of class.)

Getting Started

Write the alphabet on the board, leaving enough space for you or students to write topic ideas for each letter. Have students brainstorm science concepts they've learned throughout the year for each letter. Help them come up with concepts for the more difficult letters, such as Q, X, Y, and Z.

Inform students that they will be creating an ABC book reflecting what they've learned in science throughout the year. Invite students to choose a science concept or term for each letter of the alphabet. Explain that each page will feature one letter with a thorough explanation of a science concept that starts with that letter, examples from class and/or lab, and an illustration representing the concept. Encourage students to look over portfolios of their work for ideas.

Distribute the student handout and assign a grouping of letters, such as A–H, to be completed by a certain date. This helps pace students so they do not get overwhelmed as the deadline gets closer.

◆ ◆ ◆ ◆ ◆ ◆ ◆ **Tips** ◆ ◆ ◆ ◆ ◆ ◆ ◆

● Assign the alphabet in groups to pace students. Assign the letter groups (A–H) as a rough draft for homework so students are thinking about the concepts prior to assembling their book.

● You may want to encourage students to make this a pop-up ABC book.

Name: _____ Date: _____

The ABC's of Science

■ ■

Project Goal

Create an ABC book to demonstrate an in-depth knowledge of the concepts we have learned in science this year.

To Do

❶ List the letters of the alphabet down one side of a sheet of paper. For each letter, write a science concept you've learned this year that starts with that letter. If necessary, look back on your portfolio of work to help you.

❷ In a binder or report cover, put together 26 sheets of construction paper, one for each letter of the alphabet. Include a cover page with the title "The ABC's of Science: A Year in Review" and your name and class period.

❸ On each page you must include the following:

✔ The letter represented in a large, colorful, and creative manner

✔ The concept that the letter represents and its definition. For example:
   A is for Air Resistance. The frictional force acting against objects falling through the air.

✔ A thorough description of any lab activities done in class that demonstrate this concept

✔ An illustration of the concept

Each page should be colorful and represent something in science that we have studied this year. Major concepts from each unit covered this year must be represented. Be creative!

Due date: _____

Name: _____

■ ■ ■ ■ ■ ■ ■ **The ABC's of Science** ■ ■ ■ ■ ■ ■ ■

CRITERIA	SCORE
● Each letter of the alphabet is represented in the book.	(_____/10 points)
● Each page includes a description of the concept for that letter and its definition.	(_____/20 points)
● Each page includes a colorful and attractive illustration of the concept.	(_____/20 points)
● Each page describes a lab activity that we've done in class that demonstrates the concept.	(_____/20 points)
● The book covers all the science concepts we studied throughout the year, with each unit represented. It shows a thorough understanding of the concepts we've learned.	(_____/20 points)
● The text has been proofread and checked for spelling and grammar.	(_____/10 points)
TOTAL: _____/100 points	

Comments:

_____

_____

_____

_____

Nightly Homework GRADING RUBRIC

The following guidelines will be used to evaluate your nightly homework assignments. Your grade will take into account the quality as well as the completeness of your work.

+	• Homework is neat (e.g., no tears, wrinkles, major cross-outs, dog bites, and so on).
	• All parts of the homework are completed. (If you don't understand part of the homework, ask for help before class starts.)
	• Homework shows evidence of effort. (It does not look like it was completed hastily during recess.)
	• Homework shows creativity or originality (e.g., it includes illustrations, extra research, outstanding presentation or organization).
	• Work goes above and beyond what teacher asked for.
✔	• Homework is neat (e.g., no tears, wrinkles, major cross-outs, dog bites, and so on).
	• All parts of the homework are completed. (If you don't understand part of the homework, ask for help before class starts.)
	• Homework shows evidence of effort. (It does not look like it was completed hastily during recess.)
	• Work that the teacher asked for has been completed.
—	• Homework is only partially completed or not completed on time.
	• Homework is not done.
	• Homework is not completed by the beginning of the class on which it is due.
	• Homework is not neat.
	• Work is incomplete or not completed according to directions.

Lab Report GRADING RUBRIC

■ ■

The following rubric will be used to evaluate your understanding of concepts related to laboratory experiments. Lab reports should illustrate a thorough understanding of purpose and relation to science concepts covered in the curriculum. Relevant vocabulary and terms should be included.

PROBLEM AND HYPOTHESIS

+	Both sections are written in complete sentences. The problem is written as a question. The hypothesis is a reasonable guess.
✔	Both sections are written in complete sentences. The problem is reasonable but is not written as a question. The hypothesis is a reasonable guess.
—	One or both sections are missing or do not match the investigation.

MATERIALS

+	All important materials are clearly listed and/or pictured. The amount or number of each material is included.
✔	Most important materials are clearly listed and/or pictured. The amount or number of each material is included.
—	Important materials are not listed and/or pictured. The amount or number of each material is not included. Or, the section is missing entirely.

PROCEDURE

+	Thoroughly describes what was done in the lab. Includes details such as the materials and equipment used, how much of each material was used, how results were measured, how often results were measured, and so on. It is a detailed and accurate description of the lab, and includes at least eight sentences.
✔	Clearly describes what was done in the lab. Includes details such as the materials and equipment used but leaves out two or more specific details of how the lab was done. It is an accurate description of the lab, and includes at least five sentences.
—	Describes what was done in the lab but is missing supporting details. It is a general description of the lab and includes less than five sentences. Or, the section is missing entirely.

(continued)

Lab Report GRADING RUBRIC
(continued)

■ ■

RESULTS

+	Data charts and graphs are readable, neat, and carefully done. Graphs include a title, labels on axes, and units of measurement. Includes one or two sentences that explain what the graph/chart proves.
✔	Data charts and graphs are readable, neat, and/or carefully done. Graphs are missing one or two of the following: title, labels on axes, and units of measurement.
—	Data charts and graphs are messy and/or not carefully done. Or, graphs are missing more than two of the following: title, labels on axes, and units of measurement. Or, the section is missing entirely.

CONCLUSION

+	The question stated in the problem section has been answered. An explanation of the results and what they mean show a complete understanding and explanation of the scientific ideas involved. Key science vocabulary is used throughout the discussion.
✔	The question stated in the problem section has been answered. An explanation of the results and what they mean show a general understanding of the scientific principles involved. Some ideas may be missing or incorrect. Key science vocabulary is used in parts of the discussion.
—	The question in the problem section has been answered. An explanation of the results and what they mean show a limited understanding or no understanding of the scientific principles. Science vocabulary is not used. Or, the question is answered with no explanation. Or, the section is missing entirely.

QUESTIONS

+	Questions show a high level of originality, thought, or reflection on what the lab meant or what the student learned.
✔	Questions are present and show some level of thought and effort. Less original than a + question.
—	The questions show little effort. Or, fewer than three questions are asked.

15 Standards-Based Science Activities Kids Will Love! • Scholastic Teaching Resources